discarded

Cosmology

Understanding the Evolution of the Universe

Cosmology

Understanding the
Evolution of the Universe

Edited by Shalini Saxena

Britannica
Educational Publishing

IN ASSOCIATION WITH

ROSEN
EDUCATIONAL SERVICES

Published in 2015 by Britannica Educational Publishing (a trademark of Encyclopædia Britannica, Inc.) in association with The Rosen Publishing Group, Inc.
29 East 21st Street, New York, NY 10010

Distributed exclusively by Rosen Publishing.
To see additional Britannica Educational Publishing titles, go to rosenpublishing.com.

First Edition

Britannica Educational Publishing
J.E. Luebering: Director, Core Reference Group
Anthony L. Green: Editor, Compton's by Britannica

Rosen Publishing
Hope Lourie Killcoyne: Executive Editor
Shalini Saxena: Editor
Nelson Sá: Art Director
Brian Garvey: Designer
Cindy Reiman: Photography Manager
Karen Huang: Photo Researcher
Introduction and supplementary material by Jan Goldberg

Cataloging-in-Publication Data

Cosmology: understanding the evolution of the universe/edited by Shalini Saxena.
        pages cm.—(The study of science)
Audience: Grades 7-12.
Includes bibliographical references and index.
ISBN 978-1-62275-412-0 (library bound)
1. Cosmology—Popular works. I. Saxena, Shalini, 1982–
QB982.C67 2015
523.1—dc23

2014006450

Manufactured in the United States of America

CONTENTS

Ptolemaic diagram of a geocentric system, from the star atlas Harmonia Macrocosmica *by the cartographer Andreas Cellarius, 1660.* Photos.com/Thinkstock

ave you ever thought about how our universe came to be? Do you suppose that it happened all at once? Do you think that it evolved over time? Was there a major event that was responsible for its existence? What is the age of the universe? How big is it? What will the universe be like in the future?

The truth is, we do not have definitive answers to any of these questions. However, these questions are so important that an entire branch of astronomy, known as cosmology, is devoted to attempting to answer them. The following pages will chronicle the development of this fascinating field.

Cosmology is a branch of astronomy that specifically deals with the origin, structure, and space-time relationships of the universe. It is not the same thing as astronomy, which deals with the evolution, physics, chemistry, meteorology, and motion of celestial objects as well as the formation and development of the universe. Thus, cosmology is only one segment of astronomy. The basic assumptions of modern cosmology are that the universe is homogeneous in space (on the average, all places are alike at any time) and that the laws of physics are the same everywhere.

The first great age of scientific cosmology began in Greece in the 6th century BCE, when the Pythagoreans introduced the concept of a spherical Earth. In approximately 170 CE, one predominant theory espoused by the Greek culture (and Ptolemy of Alexandria in particular) was a geocentric one. This theory was based upon the concept that the Earth was at the center of the universe.

A number of scientists and deep thinkers offered a variety of theories over the ensuing years. Of particular significance was 16th-century astronomer Nicolaus Copernicus, who ushered in the second great age of cosmology when he developed the heliocentric concept of the solar system, which placed the Sun at the center with Earth and the other planets continually orbiting it.

Albert Einstein, one of the most brilliant scientists of the 20th century, is another individual who contributed much to our understanding of cosmology. At the top of the list was his approach to thinking about time, matter, space, energy, and gravity. He published his revolutionary theory of relativity in 1916, which marked the beginning of the third great age of cosmology.

The most popular answer to the question about how our universe came to be is known as the big bang theory. Proponents of this theory believe that between 13 and 14 billion years ago, from an infinitely hot, incredibly tiny, supercondensed state, the universe exploded. Then, in a moment following this event, the universe began expanding. For the following billions of years, the expansion continued, but at a slower pace.

Over thousands of years, the intensely hot energy mixture of the early universe began to cool down. After millions of years, gas, stars, and galaxies were formed. And in about 8 to 10 billion years, our solar system—including Earth—appeared.

Many other notable figures made substantial contributions to the world of cosmology in the 20th and 21st centuries. They include Edwin Hubble, Georges Lemaître, Aleksandre Friedmann, George Gamow, Edward Teller, Hans Bethe, Arno Penzias, Alan Guth, and George Smoot, among others. Current areas of research in cosmology include the nature of dark matter, dark energy, antimatter, and more.

After reading this book, you will see that while much about the nature and evolution of the universe remains to be discovered, the works of many individuals over the centuries have gone a long way toward answering some of our most fundamental questions.

CHAPTER 1

EARLY UNDERSTANDING

Throughout recorded history, humankind has asked big questions about the universe: How large is it? Is it finite, or does space go on forever? How old is it, or has it always been here, and will it last forever? Where in the universe are we—the center? Or does it even have a center? Is the universe fundamentally chaotic or orderly? If it is ordered, is this order constant through time? Or is it perhaps evolving, decaying, still being created, or going through cycles of creation and destruction?

The quest to find answers to such questions about the origin, history, and future of the universe and its structure and order is called cosmology. This word in fact comes from the Greek word *kosmos*, meaning "order," and "the world."

ANCIENT IDEAS

Until the last few centuries, these questions remained the province of religion and philosophy. Different cultures and traditions, at different times, offered a wide variety of answers. As for our place in the universe, a common view was the geocentric one—that Earth is at the center. This model was developed in detail by the ancient Greeks, culminating with the elaborate theory of Ptolemy of Alexandria in about 150 CE.

The Pythagoreans (5th century BCE) were responsible for one of the first Greek astronomical theories. Believing that the order of the cosmos is fundamentally mathematical, they held that it is possible to discover the harmonies of the universe by contemplating the regular motions of the heavens. Theorizing that all the heavenly bodies including the Earth and Sun revolve around a central fire, they constructed the first physical model of the solar system. Subsequent Greek astronomy derived its character from a comment ascribed to Plato, in the 4th century BCE, who is reported to have instructed the astronomers to "save the phenomena" in terms of uniform circular motion. That is to say, he urged them to develop predictively accurate theories using only combinations of uniform circular motion. As a result, Greek astronomers never regarded their geometric models as true or as being physical descriptions of the machinery

Pythagoras, believed to be the founder of the Pythagorean philosophical school, demonstrating his Pythagorean theorem in the sand using a stick. Photos.com/ Thinkstock

of the heavens. They regarded them simply as tools for predicting planetary positions.

Eudoxus of Cnidus (4th century BCE) was the first of the Greek astronomers to rise to Plato's challenge. His model consisted of a complex system of 27 interconnected spheres with Earth at the center. One sphere held the fixed stars, while each planet occupied four spheres and the Sun and Moon had three each. Using only uniform circular motions, Eudoxus was able to "save" the rather complex planetary motions with some success. The system was modified by Callippus, a student of Eudoxus's, who added spheres to improve the theory, especially for Mercury and Venus. Aristotle, in formulating his cosmology, adopted Eudoxus's homocentric spheres as the actual machinery of the heavens. The Aristotelian cosmos was like an onion consisting of a series of some 55 spheres nested about the Earth, which was fixed at the center. In order to unify the system, Aristotle added spheres in order to "unroll" the motions of a given planet so that they would not be transmitted to the next inner planet.

The theory of homocentric spheres failed to account for two sets of observations: (1) brightness changes suggesting that planets are not always the same distance from the Earth,

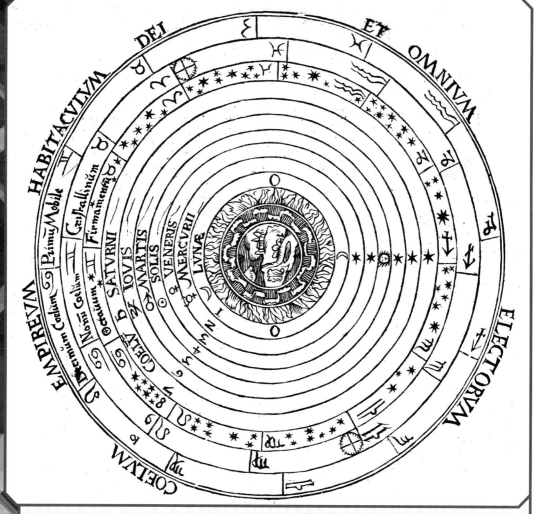

A representation of the Aristotelian cosmos, with Earth at the center. Print Collector/ Hulton Archive/Getty Images

and (2) bounded elongations (i.e., Venus is never observed to be more than about 48° and Mercury never more than about 24° from the Sun). Heracleides of Pontus (4th century BCE) attempted to solve these problems by having

Venus and Mercury revolve about the Sun, rather than the Earth, and having the Sun and other planets revolve in turn about the Earth, which he placed at the center. In addition, to account for the daily motions of the heavens, he held that the Earth rotates on its axis. Heracleides' theory had little impact in antiquity except perhaps on Aristarchus of Samos (3rd century BCE), who apparently put forth a heliocentric (Sun-centered) hypothesis similar to the one Copernicus was to propound in the 16th century.

Hipparchus (flourished 130 BCE) made extensive contributions to both theoretical and observational astronomy. Basing his theories on an impressive mass of observations, he was able to work out theories of the Sun and Moon that were more successful than those of any of his predecessors. His primary conceptual tool was the eccentric circle, a circle in which the Earth is at some point that is not the geometric center. He used this device to account for various irregularities and inequalities observed in the motions of the Sun and Moon.

Among Hipparchus's observations, one of the most significant was that of the precession of the equinoxes. Every year the Sun traces out a circular path in a west-to-east direction relative to the stars. Hipparchus had good reasons

for believing that the Sun's path, known as the ecliptic, is a great circle—that is, that the plane of the ecliptic passes through Earth's center. The two points at which the ecliptic and the equatorial plane intersect are known as the vernal and autumnal equinoxes. The two points of the ecliptic farthest north and south from the equatorial plane are known as the summer and winter solstices. The equinoxes and solstices divide the ecliptic into four equal parts, or seasons. However, the Sun's passage through each section of the ecliptic is not symmetrical. Hipparchus discovered a method of using the dates of two equinoxes and a solstice to calculate the size and direction of the displacement of the Sun's orbit. With Hipparchus's mathematical model, one could calculate not only the Sun's orbital location on any date but also its position as seen from Earth.

Hipparchus also tried to measure as precisely as possible the length of the tropical year—the period for the Sun to complete one passage through the ecliptic. He made observations of consecutive equinoxes and solstices and compared them with observations made in the 5th and 3rd centuries BCE. This led him to an estimate of the tropical year that was only 6 minutes too long.

Hipparchus observing the stars. Universal Images Group/SuperStock

Hipparchus was then able to calculate equinox and solstice dates for any year. Applying this information to observations from about 150 years before his time, he made the discovery that the positions of certain stars had shifted from the earlier measures. This indicated that Earth, not the stars, was moving. This movement, called precession, is a slow wobble in the orientation of Earth's axis caused by the gravity of the Sun and the Moon. The phenomenon discovered by Hipparchus is now known as the precession of the equinoxes.

CLAUDIUS PTOLEMY

Claudius Ptolemaeus (100?–170?), known as Ptolemy, was an eminent astronomer, mathematician, and geographer who lived in the 2nd century CE. He was of Greek descent but worked mostly in Alexandria, Egypt. In several fields his writings represent the greatest achievement of Greco-Roman science, particularly his Earth-centered model of the universe.

Almost nothing is known about Ptolemy's life except what can be inferred from his writings. He was born about 100 CE. His first major astronomical work, the *Almagest*, was completed about 150 and contains astronomical observations that Ptolemy had made over the preceding quarter of a century. The size and content of his subsequent writings suggests that he lived until about 170.

In the *Almagest* Ptolemy lays out his argument that Earth is a stationary sphere at the center of a vastly larger celestial sphere that revolves at a perfectly uniform rate around Earth. The celestial sphere carries with it the stars, the planets, the Sun, and the Moon—thereby causing their daily risings and settings. Through the course of a year the Sun slowly traces out a great orbit, the ecliptic, against the rotation of the celestial sphere. The Moon and planets similarly travel backward—thus, the planets were also known as "wandering stars"—against the "fixed stars" found in the ecliptic. The basic assumption of the *Almagest* is that the apparently irregular movements of the heavenly bodies are actually combinations of regular, uniform, circular motions. The work also provided a catalog of 1,022 stars.

Ptolemy was primarily responsible for the Earth-centered cosmology that prevailed in the Islamic world and in medieval

Europe. This was not due to the *Almagest* so much as a later treatise, *Planetary Hypotheses*. In this work he proposed what is now called the Ptolemaic system—a unified system in which each heavenly body is attached to its own sphere and the set of spheres nested so that it extends without gaps from Earth to the celestial sphere. The Ptolemaic system was the official dogma of Western Christendom until the 1500s, when it was replaced by Nicolaus Copernicus's Sun-centered system.

How much of the *Almagest* is original is difficult to determine. Ptolemy credited Hipparchus with essential elements of his solar theory, as well as parts of his lunar theory, while denying that Hipparchus constructed planetary models.

Ptolemy published several books on new geometrical proofs and theorems, prepared a calendar that gave weather indications and the rising and setting of stars, wrote five books

(continued on the next page)

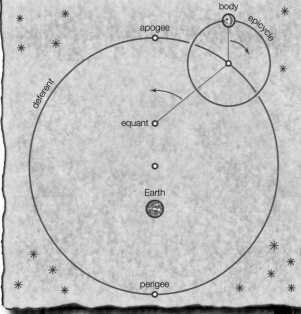

In Ptolemy's geocentric model of the universe, the Sun, the Moon, and each planet orbit a stationary Earth. For the Greeks, heavenly bodies must move in the most perfect possible fashion—hence, in perfect circles. Encyclopædia Britannica, Inc.

on optical phenomena, and developed a three-book treatise on music. His reputation as a geographer rests on his eight-volume work *Guide to Geography*. The books provide information on mapmaking and list places in Europe, Asia, and Africa by latitude and longitude. In spite of its many errors, this work greatly influenced succeeding generations of geographers and mapmakers.

Claudius Ptolemy (flourished 140 CE) compiled a systematic account of Greek astronomy. He elaborated theories for each of the planets, as well as for the Sun and Moon. His theory generally fitted the data available to him with a good degree of accuracy, and his book, the *Almagest*, became the vehicle by which Greek astronomy was transmitted to astronomers of the Middle Ages and Renaissance. It essentially molded astronomy for the next millennium and a half.

As for the history of the universe, some thinkers believed it to be eternal and unchanging. Others, perhaps inspired by such natural cycles as day and night and the seasons, thought that it was cyclic. These thinkers believed that the universe went through a series of ages,

A mandala is a symbolic diagram of the universe in Hindu and Buddhist Tantrism. Photos.com/Thinkstock

including a golden age, in which they believed themselves to be living. They believed that, after the total destruction of the universe in an age of fire, the entire cycle of ages would be repeated.

The great religious traditions of the world also have had much to say about this matter. Eastern thought, including Hinduism, generally has subscribed to the notion of cyclical time. The monotheistic traditions of Judaism,

Christianity, and Islam, however, have taken a much different view—that the universe was created at a definite time in the past and exists in much the same state until an end of some kind at a definite time in the future. Such a linear concept of time meshed well with the idea that the creator had a plan and purpose for the universe and that such a purpose would be fulfilled in the course of history.

SCIENCE APPROACHES THE PROBLEM

The advent of the methods of modern science had a huge impact on cosmological thought, beginning with the heliocentric (Sun-centered) theory of Nicolaus Copernicus in the 16th century. Perhaps the most revolutionary aspect of Copernicus's theory was that it displaced Earth from the center of the universe, making it just one of many planets orbiting the Sun. While slow to be accepted, this idea was reinforced by the work of Johannes Kepler and Galileo. It helped lead, in the late 17th century, to Isaac Newton's great synthesis of the Earth and the heavens—his theory of universal gravitation, combined with his laws of motion. Before 1600 most European thinkers had followed the ancient Greeks in conceiving

THE COPERNICAN PRINCIPLE

In the mid-16th century, Nicolaus Copernicus formulated a model of the solar system centered on the Sun, with Earth and other planets revolving around it. Published in 1543, it appeared with an introduction by Rhäticus (Rheticus) as *De revolutionibus orbium coelestium libri VI* ("Six Books Concerning the Revolutions of the Heavenly Orbs").

(continued on the next page)

A representation of the Copernican system, which places the Sun at the center of the solar system. Print Collector/Hulton Archive/Getty Images

Having the Sun in this central position explained the apparent motion of planets relative to the fixed stars and was truer than the Earth-centered Ptolemaic system. Scientifically, the Copernican system led to belief in a much larger universe than before (because, if Earth revolved around the Sun, the stars would have to be very distant not to appear to alter their position); more broadly, the Copernican principle is invoked to argue against any theory that would give the solar system a special place in the universe. Dethronement of Earth from the center of the universe caused profound shock: the Copernican system challenged the entire system of ancient authority and required a complete change in the philosophical conception of the universe.

of the Earth and the heavens as rather separate realms, with different behaviors. Newton, however, explained terrestrial and celestial motions with the same laws, including a force called gravity, which operated throughout the universe.

Newton quickly realized that gravity, which is an attraction between each body and every other body in the universe, would cause everything to collapse to a common center—if there were one. He philosophically objected to such a fate and so proposed a spatially infinite universe, with no such center defined. He was not the first to propose an infinite universe, however. Giordano Bruno had suggested this nearly a century earlier, even proposing that the stars are other suns, around which might orbit inhabited planets.

With regard to time, Newton, who considered himself a theologian as well as a scientist, relied on his Christian religious beliefs. He believed that God had created the universe at a definite time in the past, giving all bodies their initial motions. Ever since, the God-given laws of motion and gravity had directed the planets in their courses.

By the late 1800s geologists and biologists had collected evidence suggesting that the Earth was at least hundreds of millions of years old, much older than had been thought. In fact, to many it seemed

Sir Isaac Newton, portrait by John Vanderbank, c. 1725; in the collection of the Royal Astronomical Society, London. Photos.com/Thinkstock

reasonable that Earth and the universe had always existed and probably would continue into the infinite future. There were dissenting opinions, though, at least regarding the ages of the Earth and Sun. Physicists such as Lord Kelvin calculated that the Earth, apparently still molten inside, should have cooled to a solid throughout if it were more than about 40 million years old. Similarly, astronomers figured that the Sun, which was believed to shine because of energy from gravitational contraction, could not be more than a few tens of millions of years old, since it could not have sustained this output for so long without a drastic reduction in size.

The discovery of radioactivity by Henri Becquerel in 1896 led to a solution to both problems. The Earth could be heated internally by the radioactive decay of elements such as uranium, which could last billions of years. The Sun, it turned out, shines by nuclear fusion, giving it a potential lifetime of at least 10 billion years. Finally, radioactive dating of rocks indicated that the Earth was at least a few billion years old. With this new information, it again seemed that the universe could be extremely ancient, and perhaps eternal.

A common view at this point, among those scientists even considering the problem, was that the universe is infinitely large and infinitely old, with an infinity of stars. Thinkers as far back as Kepler, however, had noted a problem with this: the sky is dark at night. A simple mathematical analysis shows that in a starry universe infinite in space and time, every possible line of sight in the sky should lead eventually to the surface of a star. The entire sky thus would be brilliant, even at night.

This problem, known as Olbers' paradox (after Wilhelm Olbers, who discussed it in the 1820s), has a number of possible solutions, all of great cosmological significance. The simplest solutions are that either the universe is not infinite, or not infinitely old, or both. If, for instance, it had

Wilhelm Olbers. Print Collector/ Hulton Archive/Getty Images

a definite beginning, only those stars whose light had had time to reach Earth would be visible to us today. Interestingly, perhaps the first person to advance this argument in print was the poet Edgar Allan Poe, who wrote about it in an obscure work called "Eureka," published in 1848. Poe also suggested the possibility of an expanding universe, long before professional scientists—who probably never read the work—thought of the idea.

CHAPTER 2

COSMOLOGY IN THE EARLY 20TH CENTURY

I n 1905 Albert Einstein published his theory of special relativity, which showed that space and time can be seen as aspects of a deeper structure, space-time, and that mass and energy are really the same thing. In 1916 he followed this with his theory of general relativity, in which gravity is understood as a warping, or bending, of space-time by the presence of mass.

ALBERT EINSTEIN

Any list of the greatest thinkers in history will contain the name of the brilliant physicist Albert Einstein (1879–1955). His theories of relativity led to entirely new ways of thinking about time, space, matter, energy, and gravity. Relativity is central to modern physics. In particular, relativity provides the basis for understanding cosmic processes and the geometry of the universe itself. Einstein's work led to such scientific advances as the control of atomic

energy and to some of the investigations of space currently being made by astrophysicists.

In 1905, at age 26, he published five major research papers in an important German physics journal. He received a doctorate for the first paper. Publication of the next four papers forever changed mankind's view of the universe.

The third paper, which had its beginnings in an essay he wrote at age 16, contained the "special theory of relativity." Einstein showed that time and motion are relative to the observer, if the speed of light is constant and natural laws are the same everywhere in the universe. This paper introduced an entirely new concept. Other scientists, especially Henri Poincaré and Hendrik Lorentz, had pieces of the theory of special relativity, but Einstein was the first to assemble the whole theory together and to realize that it was a universal law of nature, not a curious figment of motion in the ether, as Poincaré and Lorentz had thought. In the 19th century there were two pillars of physics: Newton's laws of motion and James Clerk Maxwell's theory of light. Einstein was alone in realizing that they were in contradiction and that one of them must fall.

The fourth paper was a mathematical addition to the special theory of relativity. Here

Albert Einstein seated in his study. Esther Bubley/Time & Life Pictures/ Getty Images

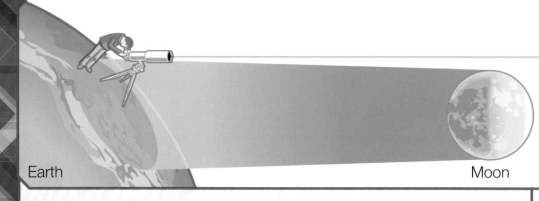

Earth   Moon

In 1919, observation of a solar eclipse confirmed Einstein's prediction that light is bent in the presence of mass. This experimental support for his general theory of relativity garnered him instant worldwide acclaim. Encyclopædia Britannica, Inc.

Einstein presented his famous formula, $E = mc^2$, known as the energy-mass relation. What it says is that the energy (E) inherent in a mass (m) equals the mass multiplied by the velocity of light squared (c^2). The formula shows that a small particle of matter is the equivalent of an enormous quantity of energy. These papers established Einstein's status among the most respected physicists in Europe.

In 1916 Einstein published his general theory of relativity. In it he proposed that gravity is not a force, a previously accepted theory, but a curved field in the space-time continuum that is created by the presence of mass. Einstein was convinced that general relativity was correct because of its mathematical

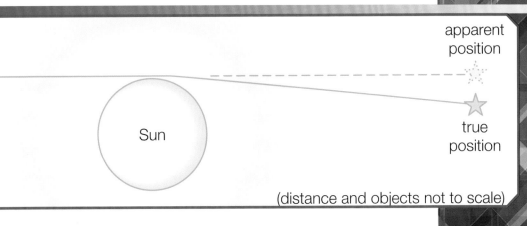

apparent
position

Sun

true
position

(distance and objects not to scale)

beauty and because it accurately predicted aspects of Mercury's orbit around the Sun.

Worldwide fame came to Einstein in 1919 when the Royal Society of London announced that predictions made in his general theory of relativity had been confirmed. He was awarded the Nobel Prize in Physics two years later; however, the prize was for his work in theoretical physics, not relativity theories, which were still considered to be controversial. When the Nazis came to power in Germany in 1933, they denounced his ideas, seized his property, and burned his books. That year he moved to the United States.

Beginning in the 1920s Einstein tried to establish a mathematical relationship between electromagnetism and gravitation. He spent the rest of his life on this unsuccessful attempt to explain all of the properties of matter and energy in a single mathematical

35

theory, called a unified field theory. A number of predictions of the general theory still await complete confirmation, including the existence of gravity waves that would be analogous to electromagnetic waves.

The singular feature of Einstein's view of gravity is its geometric nature. Whereas Newton thought that gravity was a force, Einstein showed that gravity arises from the shape of space-time. Although this is difficult to visualize, an analogy can be used to provide some insight for what is meant by the curvature of space-time without illustrating space-time itself.

The analogy begins by considering space-time as a rubber sheet that can be deformed. In any region distant from massive cosmic objects such as stars, space-time is uncurved—that is, the rubber sheet is flat. If one were to probe space-time in that region by sending out a ray of light or a test body, both the ray and the body would travel in perfectly straight lines, like a child's marble rolling across a flat rubber sheet.

However, the presence of a massive body curves space-time, as if a heavy ball were placed on the rubber sheet to create a pitlike depression. In the analogy, a marble placed near the depression rolls down the slope toward the bowling ball as if pulled by a force. In addition,

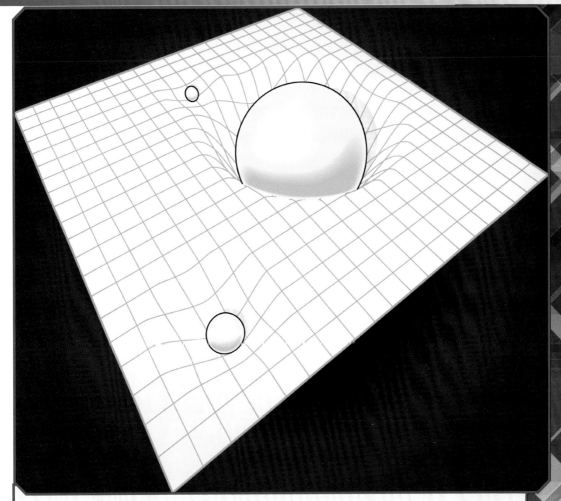

Einstein's general theory of relativity explains gravity as the curvature of space-time. This concept can be pictured by imagining space-time as a rubber sheet. The balls on the rubber sheet bend the sheet around them, somewhat as matter bends space-time in its vicinity. Encyclopædia Britannica, Inc.

if the marble is given a sideways push, it will describe an orbit around the bowling ball, as if a steady pull toward the ball is swinging the marble into a closed path.

In this way, the curvature of space-time near a star defines the shortest natural paths, or geodesics—much as the shortest path between any two points on the Earth is not a straight line, which cannot be constructed on that curved surface, but the arc of a great circle route. In Einstein's theory, space-time geodesics define the deflection of light and the orbits of planets. As the American theoretical physicist John Wheeler put it, matter tells space-time how to curve, and space-time tells matter how to move. This new theory of gravity, which has passed a number of experimental tests, paved the way for the modern scientific study of cosmology.

ANOTHER REVOLUTION IN COSMOLOGY

Einstein soon realized that his basic equations, in their simplest form, required that the universe be either expanding or contracting. Its matter—along with space itself—would be either flying apart or falling together. Einstein, like most astronomers at the time and much like Newton two centuries before, objected to such a conclusion. He favored instead the idea of a static universe, one essentially unchanging through infinite time. He realized that his equations could include a special term, called

THE COSMOLOGICAL CONSTANT

Albert Einstein reluctantly added a mathematical term called the "cosmological constant" to his equations of general relativity in order to obtain a solution to the equations that described a static universe, as he believed it to be at the time. The constant has the effect of a repulsive force that acts against the gravitational attraction of matter in the universe. When it was soon discovered that the universe is expanding, Einstein regretted having added the term to his equations. However, astronomical observations since the late 1990s have shown the existence of a repulsive force, somewhat similar in effect to the cosmological constant, which is dubbed dark energy and is the dominant component of the universe.

the cosmological constant, which could supply a sort of repulsive force, capable of balancing gravity and keeping the universe static. While it might be simpler to leave it out (by assigning it a value of zero), Einstein assigned it a positive value so that the universe would be essentially unchanging, as he expected.

THE EXPANDING UNIVERSE

In 1929, however, Edwin Hubble announced an amazing discovery—evidence that the universe actually is expanding. In the mid-1920s

Edwin Hubble. Roth Sanford/Photo Researchers/Getty Images

astronomers had found that a class of cloud-like objects, then called spiral nebulae, are actually huge, distant groups of billions of stars, now called galaxies. Hubble's analysis of their light showed that, with the exception of a few of the closest ones, they are all moving away from Earth, many at tremendous speeds. When Einstein realized that he had held in his hands the monumental prediction of a universe evolving through time and had then undone it with the cosmological constant, he called it the "greatest blunder" of his life.

EDWIN POWELL HUBBLE

A U.S. astronomer, Edwin Powell Hubble (1889–1953) played a crucial role in establishing the field of extragalactic astronomy—the study of objects outside the Milky Way Galaxy. He is generally regarded as the leading astronomer of the 20th century. The Hubble Space Telescope was named after him.

Hubble was born in Marshfield, Missouri, on November 20, 1889. In 1910 he graduated from the University of Chicago and was selected as a Rhodes Scholar. He spent three years at the University of Oxford and was awarded a B.A. in jurisprudence, a subject he had taken at the insistence of his father. After his father's death in 1913, the way was open for him to pursue a scientific career. He returned to the United States and began graduate studies in astronomy at the University of Chicago.

After serving in the U.S. Army during World War I, Hubble earned his doctorate and went to work with his former teacher, George Hale, at the Mount Wilson Observatory in California. There he observed spiral nebulae, objects he had investigated for his doctorate. The status of these objects was then unclear. It was unknown whether they were distant star systems comparable to the Milky Way Galaxy or clouds of gas or sparse star clusters within, or close to, the Milky Way.

In 1923 Hubble found a type of star called Cepheid variables in the Andromeda Nebula, a very well-known spiral. He used the fluctuations in light of these stars to determine the nebula's distance. He determined that the nebula was several hundred thousand light-years away (outside the Milky Way Galaxy) and that it was actually another galaxy. Hubble's finds in the Andromeda Nebula and in other

(continued on the next page)

relatively nearby spiral nebulae swiftly convinced the great majority of astronomers that the universe in fact contains many galaxies.

In studying galaxies in 1927 Hubble made his second remarkable discovery: that the galaxies were receding from the Milky Way at rates that increased with distance. This implied that the universe, long considered unchanging, was expanding. Even more remarkable, the ratio of the galaxies' speed to their distance was a constant, named Hubble's constant in his honor. Hubble's original calculation of the constant was incorrect: it made the Milky Way larger than

Image of the Andromeda Galaxy taken by NASA's Wide-field Infrared Survey Explorer (WISE). Blue indicates mature stars, while yellow and red show dust heated by newborn massive stars. NASA/JPL-Caltech/UCLA

all other galaxies and the entire universe younger than the surmised age of Earth. Later astronomers determined that galaxies were systematically more distant, resolving the discrepancy. Hubble died in San Marino, California, on September 28, 1953.

To determine the distances to other galaxies, Hubble compared the brightness of certain giant stars in these galaxies to the brightness of presumably similar stars in our own galaxy, whose distances had been calculated by a number of other, overlapping methods. To determine the speed at which a galaxy was receding from Earth, he observed its spectrum. Dark lines in the spectrum of colors can be identified as being produced by specific chemical elements known on Earth. For these galaxies, the lines were shifted away from their normal wavelengths toward the red, long-wavelength part of the spectrum.

This effect is known as redshift. It is similar to the Doppler effect for sound, in which, for instance, a train whistle's pitch seems to drop as the train passes by. The sound waves from the receding train whistle are stretched out behind the train and arrive at the listener with

The Doppler Shift

Absorption lines from an approaching object shift toward the violet (shorter wavelength).

The amount of shift depends on the velocity of the object in relationship to the observer: the greater the velocity, the greater the shift.

Absorption lines from the Sun are used for comparison.

Absorption lines from a receding object shift toward the red (longer wavelength).

The Doppler effect. Encyclopædia Britannica, Inc.

a longer wavelength and thus a lower pitch. The wavelengths of light from a receding object are likewise stretched longer, making the light appear redder than it would otherwise.

Hubble plotted recessional speeds of galaxies versus their distance from Earth and

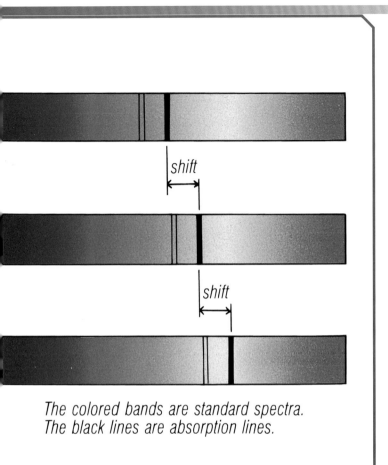

The colored bands are standard spectra.
The black lines are absorption lines.

found that the more distant ones were moving away at proportionally greater speeds,
so that the graph formed nearly a straight
line. This relation is known as Hubble's law.
It can be written $v = H \times d$, where v is the
velocity of recession, d is the distance to the
galaxy, and H is the slope of the line and is
called Hubble's constant. According to this,
for example, a galaxy twice as far away from

an observer as another galaxy is moving away from the observer twice as fast.

It is important to realize that this expansion is best thought of not as galaxies rushing away from each other through preexisting space but rather as an expansion of space itself, which "carries" the galaxies with it. With this in mind, the redshift can be considered as the effect of space having stretched since the light was emitted. Light emitted when the universe was half its current size, for example, would now be seen to have twice the original wavelength.

THE UNIFORM UNIVERSE

The distribution of the galaxies Hubble studied also provided evidence of the cosmological principle—two important properties that the universe is assumed to have. At large scales the universe is isotropic, or looks about the same in all directions, and homogeneous, or is about the same everywhere. If the positions of vast numbers of galaxies were plotted to form a map of the observable universe, their large-scale distribution would look roughly the same from all angles and in all regions.

This means that, even though we see other galaxies rushing away from us, we cannot claim

A picture taken by the Hubble Space Telescope shows a group of four galaxies and other stars. The Hubble Heritage Team (AURA/STScI/NASA)

to be located in the "center"; an observer anywhere in the universe would see about the same thing. Every cluster of galaxies, including ours, is receding from all others as space expands. This is in many ways an extension of the Copernican notion of Earth's location in the cosmos being typical, rather than unique or privileged.

CHAPTER 3

LOOKING BACKWARD: THE BIG BANG

Hubble's findings about the expansion of the universe have a very interesting implication. If the motion of the galaxies is traced back in time, it implies that they were once all in the same place—"here." The universe would have then been greatly compressed and therefore very dense and hot. Assuming a constant rate of expansion, modern values of this constant imply that this state existed some 13 to 14 billion years ago, though calculations that include gravitational slowing of the expansion make it a bit more recent. This scenario—of a universe that "exploded" out of an extremely tiny, dense, and hot initial state—became known as the big bang theory. In the 1920s Georges Lemaître and Aleksandr Friedmann proposed early versions of such a model, which George Gamow and other cosmologists modified in the 1940s.

The big bang model is based on two assumptions. The first is that Albert Einstein's general theory of relativity

FRIEDMANN-LEMAÎTRE AND GAMOW MODELS

In 1922 Aleksandr A. Friedmann, a Russian meteorologist and mathematician, and in 1927 Georges Lemaître, a Belgian cleric, independently discovered solutions to Einstein's equations that contained realistic amounts of matter. These evolutionary models correspond to big bang cosmologies. Friedmann and Lemaître adopted Einstein's assumption of spatial homogeneity and isotropy (the cosmological principle). They rejected, however, his assumption of time independence and considered both positively curved spaces ("closed" universes) as well as negatively curved spaces ("open" universes). The difference between the approaches of Friedmann and Lemaître is that the former set the cosmological constant equal to zero, whereas the latter retained the possibility that it might have a nonzero value.

Nuclear physicist George Gamow was a proponent of the expanding-universe theory that had been advanced by Friedmann, Lemaître, and Edwin Hubble. Gamow, however, modified the theory, and he and Ralph Alpher published this theory in a paper called "The Origin of Chemical Elements" (1948). As a joke, Gamow added the name of physicist Hans Bethe to the paper in order to create the name sequence of "Alpher-Bethe-Gamow," which resembled the sequence of the first three letters of the Greek alphabet: alpha, beta, gamma. Only one page in length, the paper attempted to explain the distribution of chemical elements throughout the universe and posits a primeval thermonuclear explosion, the big bang that began the universe. According to the theory, after the big bang, atomic nuclei were built up by the successive capture of neutrons by the initially formed pairs and triplets.

George Gamow. Carl Iwasaki/Time & Life Pictures/Getty Images

correctly describes the gravitational interaction of all matter. The second assumption, the cosmological principle, states that an observer's view of the universe depends neither on the location of the observation or the direction in which it is made. This principle applies only to the large-scale properties of the universe, but it does imply that the universe has no edge, so that the big bang origin occurred not at a particular point in space but rather throughout space at the same time. These two assumptions make it possible to calculate the history of the universe after an extremely brief initial period called the Planck time. Scientists have yet to determine what prevailed before Planck time.

Tracing the expansion of the universe back toward its presumed origin can be thought of as like playing a movie backward. As one "rewinds," one finds the universe's average temperature increasing, much like that of a gas being compressed. At an age of a few hundred thousand years, the temperature would have been thousands of degrees Fahrenheit or Celsius, thus stripping atoms of their electrons. If one could have witnessed this state, there would have been a brilliant glow coming from all directions. Calculations show that at about a second after the beginning, temperatures would have been billions of degrees.

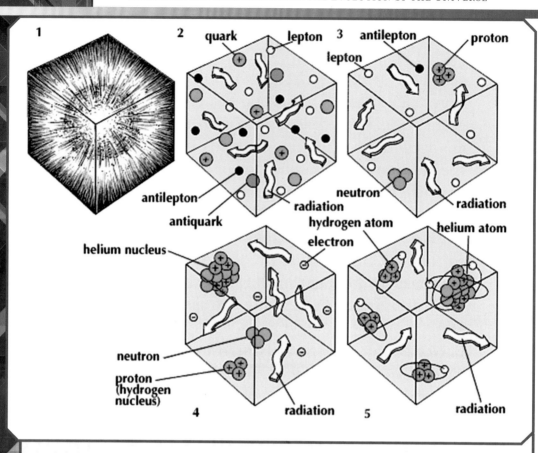

(1) The big bang. (2) Quarks and leptons and their antiparticle equivalents filled the universe. (3) By 0.01 seconds after the big bang, some quarks united to form neutrons and protons. (4) After 3.5 minutes hydrogen and helium nuclei had formed. (5) After a million years, the universe was populated with hydrogen and helium atoms.
Encyclopædia Britannica, Inc.

Under such conditions the nuclei of atoms would be smashed apart into their constituent neutrons and protons. At even earlier times, neutrons and protons would be broken up into the quarks of which they are made. These would be embedded in a soup of radiation—mainly gamma rays—along with electrons and positrons.

PREDICTIONS OF THE BIG BANG THEORY

Two crucial predictions emerge from this scenario. Playing the movie forward again, one finds that in the rapidly cooling universe, only a fraction of the protons and neutrons would have had time to fuse together to form elements heavier than hydrogen, which has only one proton. Calculations show that, by the time this fusion ended about a few minutes after the beginning, the cooling gas would have consisted of nearly 75 percent hydrogen, about 25 percent helium, and trace amounts of deuterium and lithium. One would expect this primordial 3:1 hydrogen-to-helium ratio to dominate the universe even today.

The second prediction involves the light produced by the radiant heat of the early universe. Before the formation of atoms, the particles of light, called photons, frequently scattered off of electrons, which were not yet incorporated into atoms. As atoms formed about 400,000 years after the beginning, the light finally had a clear path. Light that was thus released at a great distance should just now be reaching us. It would be coming from parts of the universe receding from us at nearly the speed of light, so that it would be

ANTIMATTER

In 1928 British theoretical physicist P.A.M. Dirac claimed that a particle of the same mass as an electron but having a positive charge could exist. Four years later a positive electron, or positron, was detected. This was the first experimental evidence for the existence of antimatter. If a particle possesses an electrical charge, its antiparticle possesses an equal but opposite charge. Particle physicists now assume that for every type of subatomic particle that occurs in nature a corresponding antiparticle exists, even if the antiparticle has not been observed. An antiparticle may be discovered years after its corresponding type of particle. Scientists have also created antiatoms, which are made up of antiparticles.

An important property of matter is demonstrated when an electron and a positron meet. They annihilate one another. Both particles disappear. The law of conservation of mass-energy states that if mass is destroyed an equivalent amount of energy must be created, so that the sum of mass-energy before and after annihilation are exactly equal.

This is precisely what happens. When an electron and a positron annihilate each other, a large amount of energy, corresponding to the mass of the two particles, is always given off. Similar annihilations occur when other types of particles meet their antiparticles.

A converse to the process of particle-antiparticle annihilation is known as pair production, in which radiation disappears and matter is created. The most common example is the creation of an electron-positron pair from a photon. For this to occur, a minimum photon energy, corresponding to two electron masses, is necessary.

Although positrons are readily created in the collisions of cosmic rays, there is no evidence for the existence of large

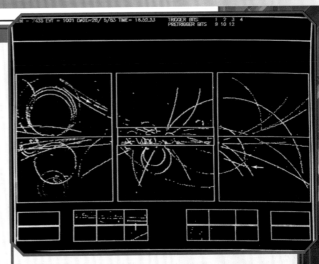

amounts of antimatter in the universe. The Milky Way Galaxy appears to consist entirely of matter, as there are no indications for regions where matter and antimatter meet and annihilate to produce characteristic gamma rays. The implication that matter completely dominates antimatter in the universe appears to be in con-

Tracks of an energetic, oppositely directed electron-positron pair (arrows), are identified in the record of a spray of debris from a proton-antiproton collision at CERN, in Geneva, Switzerland. Center horizontal lines indicate the paths of the colliding beams. Courtesy of CERN

tradiction to Dirac's theory, which, supported by experiment, shows that particles and antiparticles are always created in equal numbers from energy. The energetic conditions of the early universe should have created equal numbers of particles and antiparticles; mutual annihilation of particle-antiparticle pairs, however, would have left nothing but energy. In the universe today, photons (energy) outnumber protons (matter) by a factor of one billion. This suggests that most of the particles created in the early universe were indeed annihilated by antiparticles, while one in a billion particles had no matching antiparticle and so survived to form the matter observed today in stars and galaxies. The tiny imbalance between particles and antiparticles in the early universe is referred to as matter-antimatter asymmetry, and its cause remains a major unsolved puzzle for cosmology and particle physics.

greatly redshifted, all the way into the microwave region of the spectrum. This microwave glow should be coming from all directions in the sky, with almost uniform intensity.

EVIDENCE FOR THE BIG BANG THEORY

The first of these predictions was quickly supported by spectroscopic studies. Indeed, the visible matter in the universe does appear to be mostly hydrogen and helium, in about a 3:1 ratio, with only small amounts of heavier elements. However, the existence of most elements heavier than helium, such as what the Earth—and people—are made of, required an explanation. This was soon accounted for by studies of fusion reactions that power the stars. Stars produce heavier elements in their cores, and some of these stars explode or otherwise expel matter, enriching the universe with a fairly small but significant amount of matter heavier than helium.

Interestingly, the term *big bang* was originally intended as a derisive one; it was coined in the 1940s by Fred Hoyle, who championed a competing model known as the steady-state theory. In that model, the universe is expanding, but its general appearance and

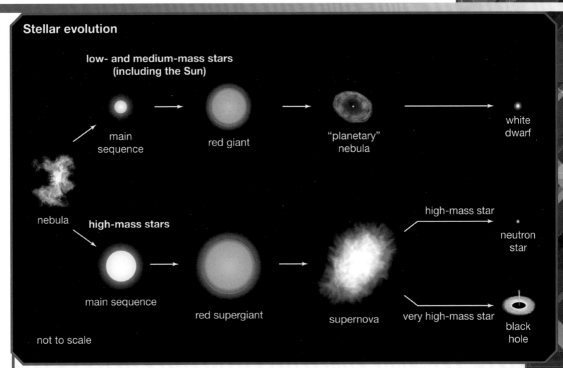

Stellar evolution

low- and medium-mass stars
(including the Sun)

main sequence

red giant

"planetary" nebula

white dwarf

nebula

high-mass stars

main sequence

red supergiant

supernova

high-mass star

neutron star

very high-mass star

black hole

not to scale

The evolution of a star depends on its mass. Low- and medium-mass stars, such as the Sun, ultimately end up as white dwarfs. High-mass stars become neutron stars, while the highest-mass stars end up as black holes. Encyclopædia Britannica, Inc.

composition remain constant through time, as new matter is gradually created to fill in the gaps left by matter that has spread out. A steady-state universe has no beginning or end in time, and from any point within it the view on the grand scale—that is, the average density and arrangement of galaxies—is the same. The universe would be infinitely old and would last forever. Galaxies of all possible ages are intermingled. The theory was advanced in 1948 by Hermann Bondi and Thomas Gold. It was further developed by Sir Fred Hoyle to

COSMIC BACKGROUND EXPLORER (COBE)

The Cosmic Background Explorer (COBE) is a U.S. satellite placed in Earth orbit in 1989 to map the "smoothness" of the cosmic background radiation field and, by extension, to confirm the validity of the big bang theory of the origin of the universe.

In 1964 Arno Penzias and Robert Wilson, working together at Bell Laboratories in New Jersey to calibrate a large microwave antenna prior to using it to monitor radio-frequency emissions from space, discovered the presence of microwave radiation that seemed to permeate the cosmos uniformly. Now known as the cosmic background radiation, this uniform field provided spectacular support for the big bang model, which held that the early universe was very hot and the subsequent expansion of the universe would redshift the thermal radiation of the early universe to much longer wavelengths corresponding to much cooler thermal radiation. Penzias

Robert Wilson (left) *and Arno Penzias standing in front of the antenna that helped them discover faint electromagnetic radiation.* Ted Thai/Time & Life Pictures/Getty Images

and Wilson shared a Nobel Prize in Physics in 1978 for their discovery, but, in order to test the theory of the early history of the universe, cosmologists needed to know whether the radiation field was isotropic (that is, the same in every direction) or anisotropic (that is, having spatial variation).

The 4,900-pound (2,200-kilogram) COBE satellite was launched by the National Aeronautics and Space Administration on a Delta rocket on Nov. 18, 1989, to make these fundamental observations. COBE's Far Infrared Absolute Spectrophotometer (FIRAS) was able to measure the spectrum of the radiation field 100 times more accurately than had previously been possible using balloon-borne detectors in Earth's atmosphere, and in so doing it confirmed that the spectrum of the radiation precisely matched what had been predicted by the theory. The Differential Microwave Radiometer (DMR) produced an all-sky survey that showed "wrinkles" indicating that the field was isotropic to 1 part in 100,000. Although this may seem minor, the fact that the big bang gave rise to a universe that was slightly denser in some places than in others would have stimulated gravitational separation and, ultimately, the formation of galaxies. COBE's Diffuse Infrared Background Experiment measured radiation from the formation of the earliest galaxies. After four years of observations, the COBE mission was ended, but the satellite remained in orbit.

In 2006 John Mather, COBE project scientist and FIRAS team leader, and George Smoot, DMR principal investigator, won the Nobel Prize in Physics for the FIRAS and DMR results.

address issues that had arisen with the alternative big bang hypothesis. For a decade or so, mainly in the 1950s, the steady-state theory enjoyed significant support.

Discoveries in the 1960s, however, weighed heavily against the steady-state theory. Especially groundbreaking was evidence in 1965 to support the other crucial prediction

The COBE satellite. Science & Society Picture Library/Getty Images

of the big bang theory: a nearly uniform glow of microwaves is indeed coming from every direction in the sky. Eventually satellite observations, including those from the Cosmic Background Explorer (COBE) launched in 1989, showed that the spectrum of this radiation was of the type known as a blackbody spectrum, which is the kind expected to result from a hot, glowing gas such as that of the early universe. Furthermore, its wavelength (about 0.4 inches [1 centimeter], which corresponds to a temperature of only about 3 Kelvin [-454°F, or -270°C]) matched closely calculations of just how redshifted this light should be now. This "wall of light," called the cosmic background radiation, is exactly what the big bang model predicts, so the theory gained very wide acceptance.

In addition to accounting for the presence of ordinary matter and radiation, the big bang model predicts that the present universe should also be filled with neutrinos, fundamental particles with no mass or electric charge. The possibility exists that other relics from the early universe may eventually be discovered.

Although it has few adherents today, the steady-state theory is credited as having been

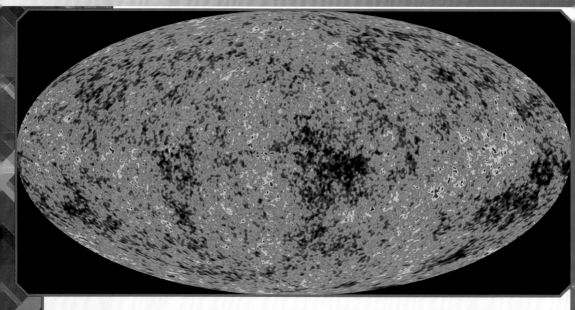

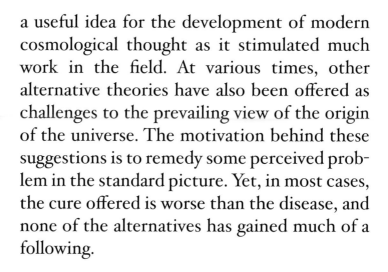

An image produced by the Wilkinson Microwave Anisotropy Probe (WMAP) showing cosmic background radiation, a very uniform glow of microwaves emitted by the infant universe more than 13 billion years ago. Color differences indicate tiny fluctuations in the intensity of the radiation, a result of tiny variations in the density of matter in the early universe. Science & Society Picture Library/Getty Images

a useful idea for the development of modern cosmological thought as it stimulated much work in the field. At various times, other alternative theories have also been offered as challenges to the prevailing view of the origin of the universe. The motivation behind these suggestions is to remedy some perceived problem in the standard picture. Yet, in most cases, the cure offered is worse than the disease, and none of the alternatives has gained much of a following.

CHAPTER 4

LOOKING FORWARD: THE FATE OF THE UNIVERSE

C osmologists of the 20th century had also been considering how the universe might develop in the future. In the 1920s Russian mathematician and physical scientist Aleksandr Friedmann had used general relativity to develop a set of models representing three possible universes with the cosmological constant set to zero. One possibility is a universe that would expand for a time but eventually collapse back to a very dense state. Such a universe would be finite in volume and yet have no edges, a condition called closed. Its geometry is described as having "positive" curvature, somewhat like the surface of a sphere. Another possibility is an open universe, which would expand forever and be infinite in size. Its geometry would have a "negative" curvature, somewhat like a saddle. A third possibility is that the universe might be precisely balanced on the line between open and closed. Its space would be flat, with no net overall curvature. A flat universe (with no cosmological constant)

Models of the Size of the Universe over Time

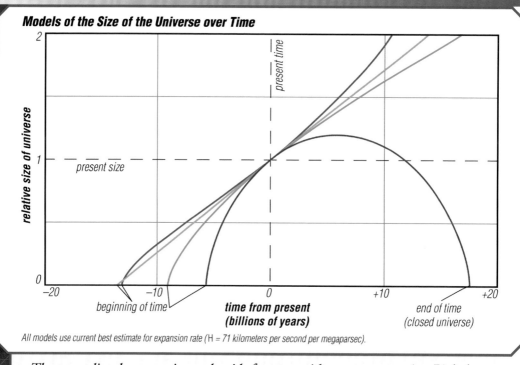

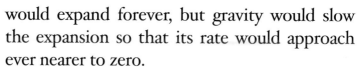

All models use current best estimate for expansion rate (H = 71 kilometers per second per megaparsec).

The orange line shows a universe devoid of matter, with constant expansion. Pink shows a collapsing universe, with six times the critical density of matter. Green shows a model favored until 1998, with exactly the critical density and a universe 100 percent matter. Blue shows the currently favored scenario, with exactly the critical density, of which 27 percent is visible and dark matter and 73 percent is dark energy. Encyclopædia Britannica, Inc.

would expand forever, but gravity would slow the expansion so that its rate would approach ever nearer to zero.

The deciding factor between these fates is the universe's density of matter and energy. The density needed to render space flat is called the critical density. With a density greater than this, the mutual gravitational attraction of all matter in the universe would slow the expansion enough to stop it and then lead to collapse.

In other words, the universe would be closed. With less than critical density, however, the attraction would also slow the expansion but not enough to ever reverse it. In that case the universe would expand forever and be open.

DIFFICULTIES AND THEIR SOLUTIONS

Many astronomers have been attracted to the idea of a flat universe, for a variety of reasons. For one, for the universe to be even remotely near critical density today, it must have been astonishingly close to critical density early in its history. It seems odd to many to have something be so nearly perfect without being absolutely perfect. Studies of the amount of visible matter in the universe, however, suggested that there was not nearly enough to render the universe flat.

Furthermore, for the universe to be anywhere close to flat today within the standard big bang model, it had to have been "fine-tuned" to astonishing precision very early in time. At one second after the big bang, for instance, had the matter in the universe been a billionth of a percentage point over the critical density, the universe would have quickly collapsed in a "big crunch." Had it been less

dense by a similar amount, the universe would have expanded so quickly that galaxies as we know them could never have formed.

The remarkably smooth nature of the universe observed today—that it is roughly the same in all regions and all directions—also is difficult to explain with the standard big bang model. Early in that model, parts of the universe widely separated from each other would not have had time to have been in contact with each other via the fastest signal known: light. For example, the temperature of the cosmic background radiation in different far-flung regions of the universe is very nearly the same. How did this occur without these regions ever communicating? Without such communication to provide the uniformity in a natural way, the early expansion of the universe would have to have been extremely well "choreographed." While one can simply suppose that the conditions were just right, a more natural explanation would be very desirable.

INFLATION

Inflation theory, a modification of the big bang theory developed by Alan Guth and others from about 1980, provided possible solutions to a couple of these problems. In inflation theory, at only a tiny fraction of a second after the start of expansion, the rapidly cooling universe became "trapped" in a state called a false vacuum. Such a state has the curious effect of making gravity a repulsive, rather than attractive, force. This propelled the early universe into an extremely fast expansion. This rapid expansion flattened space and also allowed regions already in communication to become spread over vast regions, thus explaining the high degree of uniformity seen today. After this, the universe underwent a dramatic transition to a true vacuum, releasing vast amounts of energy that reheated the universe and eventually condensed into all the matter seen today.

Evolutionary Theory of the Universe

Billions of Years Later

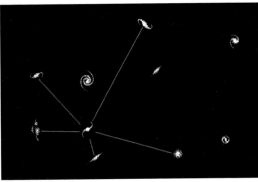

Now

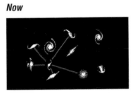

At left is a two-dimensional representation of the universe as it appears now, with galaxies occupying a typical section of space. At right, billions of years later the same amount of matter will fill a larger volume of space. Encyclopædia Britannica, Inc.

67

Although inflation produces a broadly uniform universe, it also predicts a fairly specific amount of irregularity—about the amount needed to serve as seeds for the gravitational clustering that led to the formation of galaxies. This clumpiness is a natural result of quantum mechanics, which predicts that even in a vacuum, tiny, rapid fluctuations in local energy occur all the time. Inflation would suddenly expand these microscopic irregularities so greatly that they would be the size of galaxies today, leaving their greatly magnified imprint on the cosmos. In 1992 the COBE satellite detected small temperature fluctuations in the cosmic background radiation, thus adding support to the inflationary scenario.

Most cosmologists accept some version of inflation as part of the overall big bang picture, though some of the details of inflation are still unclear. (It is hoped, for example, that the false vacuum state will be shown to be a natural prediction of particle physics, but at the moment the underlying theories do not seem complete.) Inflation extends the account of the universe's history back to only 10^{-35} (1 divided by a 1 followed by 35 zeros) second after the beginning of time. Before that, the picture becomes blurred, and at 10^{-43} (called Planck time) it is very uncertain, since conditions were so extreme that current theories of gravity and quantum mechanics are believed to be inadequate.

DARK MATTER

In the late 20th century perhaps the most important question facing cosmologists was whether the universe had critical density. Surveys of visible matter in the universe fell far short, with only about 1 percent of the necessary mass. However, studies of velocities of stars in galaxies and of galaxies in clusters

Composite image showing the galaxy cluster 1E0657-56, the Bullet cluster. X-ray: NASA/CXC/CfA/M.Markevitch Optical: NASA/STScI; Magellan/U.Arizona/D.Clowe Lensing Map: NASA/STScI; ESO WFI; Magellan/U.Arizona/D.Clowe

had shown that more matter must be present. Their speeds were often so high that more gravity—and apparently more mass—was required to keep them from flying apart. This unseen matter was dubbed dark matter, and it seems to exist in at least two forms. Some of it surely consists of well-understood objects

WIMPs

Weakly interacting massive particles (WIMPs) are theoretical particles that may help to explain the discrepancy between how much total mass is expected to exist in the galaxies and how much is actually accounted for by adding up the mass of the known cosmic matter. It is hypothesized that WIMPs make up most dark matter and therefore some 22 percent of the universe. They are invisible because they are not illuminated by any celestial light source, yet their mass may be 10 times greater than the mass of a proton.

These particles are thought to be heavy and slow moving because if the dark matter particles were light and fast moving, they would not have clumped together in the density fluctuations from which galaxies and clusters of galaxies formed. The absence of light from these particles also indicates that they are electromagnetically neutral. WIMPs are assumed to be "nonbaryonic," or something other than baryons (massive particles such as the proton and neutron that are made up of three quarks), because the amount of baryons in the universe has been determined by measuring the abundance of elements heavier than hydrogen that were created in the first few minutes after the big bang. The precise nature of these particles is not currently known, and they are not predicted by the standard model of particle physics.

Extraordinary efforts are under way to detect and measure the properties of these unseen WIMPs, either by witnessing their impact in a laboratory detector or by observing their annihilations after they collide with each other. There is also some expectation that their presence and mass may be inferred from experiments at particle accelerators such as the Large Hadron Collider.

The magnetic core of the Compact Muon Solenoid magnet at CERN in Geneva, Switzerland, preparing to take data at the Large Hadron Collider. Fabrice Coffrini/ AFP/Getty Images

such as undetected planets, brown dwarfs (bodies just short of having enough mass to become stars), neutron stars, and black holes. Still, these objects and visible matter together probably make up less than 5 percent of the critical density.

Computer simulations of early galaxy formation seem to require additional matter, though, to provide enough gravitation to produce the clustering of galaxies seen today. These simulations work well only when this matter is "cold," meaning that its particles are moving slowly relative to each other. This cold dark matter is not made of protons and neutrons like ordinary matter. It is thought to account for another 20–25 percent of the critical density. All together, these types of matter likely provide about 25–30 percent of the needed mass and therefore seemed to leave the universe open and destined to expand forever.

DARK ENERGY AND THE RUNAWAY UNIVERSE

Another problem was brewing, though. By the mid-1990s, data flowing in from several sources, including the Hubble Space Telescope, allowed newly refined values of the Hubble constant. When applied to models of the universe with anywhere near the critical density, the new estimates of this constant gave a universe no more than about 10 billion years old. Estimates of the ages of the oldest stars continued to be at least 12 billion years. Some cosmologists began to reluctantly consider Einstein's abandoned cos-

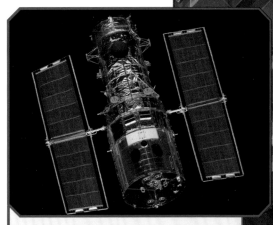

The Hubble Space Telescope appears in a photograph taken from the space shuttle Discovery *in December 1999.* NASA

mological constant, this time not to make the universe completely static, but rather to buy it more time so that it could indeed contain objects as old as these oldest stars.

Astronomers conducted two separate studies in 1998, basically to extend Hubble's graph to unprecedented distances. It was hoped that these would help pin down the rate at which the universe's expansion was slowing down and thus determine its ultimate fate, independently of surveys attempting to find dark matter. The two studies used observations of a type of supernova—a class of brilliant exploding stars of rather predictable brightness, observable even in distant galaxies. By relating the distances to such supernovae (determined from their apparent brightness) with the observed speeds of their recession, a history of the universe's expansion rate can be determined.

The results were very surprising. Distant supernovae appeared fainter than expected,

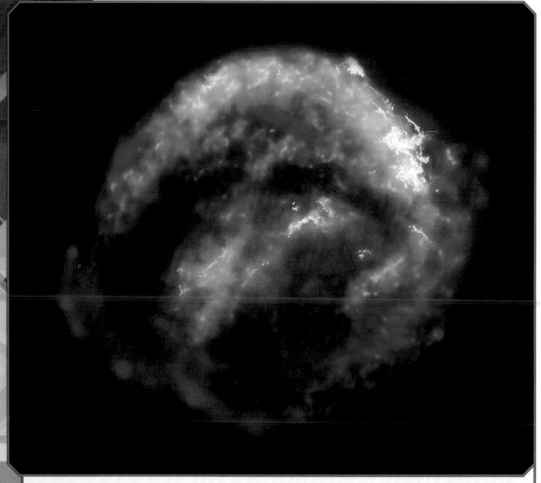

Composite image of Kepler's Nova, or Kepler's Supernova, taken by the Chandra X-ray Observatory. NASA, ESA, R. Sankrit and W. Blair, Johns Hopkins University

considering the amount of redshift of their light. If a galaxy appears surprisingly faint, it must be surprisingly far away. The light thus must have taken surprisingly long to get here. Since the redshift indicates how much the universe has expanded since the light was emitted, this means that the universe took surprisingly long to reach its current size. The universe must have been expanding more slowly in the past. These results indicated that the expansion is actually speeding up. Extensive checking of the results confirmed the finding, and now it is widely accepted that the universe is somehow blowing itself apart.

The question immediately arose as to how this could happen, since gravity is an attractive force and should be slowing the expansion. The answer is that, apparently, some kind of cosmic repulsive force is at work. Unlike gravity, whose strength diminishes with distance, this force apparently grows in strength with distance. Cosmologists quickly recognized that Einstein's cosmological constant would produce just such an effect.

Although the cosmological constant nicely describes this new force, it does not clearly specify its origin or nature. Cosmologists have scrambled to provide a physical basis for its existence and have proposed a number of ideas.

The leading contender at present appears to be "dark energy," which fills the cosmos and provides a sort of negative pressure to drive the accelerated expansion. It now seems that this dark energy makes up about 70–75 percent of the universe's mass/energy content. This would supply the needed energy to reach

The main telescope of the Sloan Digital Sky Survey (SDSS) at the Apache Point Observatory in Sunspot, New Mexico. Fermilab/Science Source

the critical density, so the universe would be flat. Despite the strangeness of this discovery, the good news is that with slower expansion in the past, the model yields a universe 13–14 billion years old, which can accommodate the oldest stars.

Using the latest information on the expansion rate and the various mass and energy densities in the universe, cosmologists have constructed computer models to study how matter and radiation interacted in the early universe. These models make very specific predictions about the amount of clustering in stars, galaxies, and clusters and superclusters of galaxies. To check these predictions, astronomers have undertaken exhaustive mapping efforts—such as the Sloan Digital Sky Survey, the 2dF (Two-Degree Field) surveys, and the Wilkinson Microwave Anisotropy Probe (WMAP)—to find the actual distribution of matter in the universe. The results so far appear to fit the theories very well indeed, adding to scientists' confidence that their overall picture of an accelerating inflationary big bang universe is at least close to the truth.

CONCLUSION

Huge advances in our understanding of the cosmos have come in recent years, but many questions remain. Will the big bang scenario continue to account for the flood of new data on the universe's structure? What is the nature of the mysterious dark energy, and will it really produce eternal expansion? What exactly caused cosmological inflation, and will this scenario be supported by more complete theories of particle physics? Will a hoped-for theory of quantum gravity be able to describe the universe at its earliest instants? What caused the universe to come into existence in the first place, and are there other such universes? Some of these questions may never be answered with certainty, but cosmologists will continue to seek answers. If history is any indicator, surprises may well await us.

annihilate To destroy completely.

antimatter Matter composed of antiparticles.

antiparticle A subatomic particle, such as a positron, antiproton, or antineutron, that possesses certain properties that are opposite those of ordinary subatomic particles of the same mass.

asymmetry Displaying a lack of proportion.

calibrate To measure precisely; especially, to measure against a standard.

celestial Of or relating to the sky or visible heavens.

concentric Having a common center.

continuum A continuous extent, succession, or whole, no part of which can be distinguished from neighboring parts except by arbitrary division.

ecliptic The great circle of the celestial sphere on which the Sun appears to move among the stars.

electromagnetism Magnetism developed by a current of electricity; a natural force arising from interactions between charged particles.

geocentric Having or relating to the Earth as center.

heliocentric Pertaining to the presence of the Sun at the center, or appearing as if seen from the Sun.

hypothesis A tentative assumption made in order to draw out and test its logical or empirical consequences.

isotropic Exhibiting properties (as velocity of light transmission) with the same values when measured along axes in all directions.

linear Of, relating to, resembling, or having a graph that is a straight line: involving a single dimension.

nebula A group of stars that is very far away and looks like a bright cloud at night.

paradox Something (such as a situation) that is made up of two opposite things and that seems impossible but is actually true or possible.

postulate To assume or claim as true, existent, or necessary.

primeval Of or relating to the earliest ages (as of the world or human history).

quark Any of several elementary particles that are believed to be components of protons, neutrons, and certain other heavy subatomic particles.

spectrum The entire range of wavelengths or frequencies of electromagnetic waves extending from gamma rays to the longest radio waves and including visible light.

subatomic Smaller than an atom; of or relating to the inside of an atom.

subsequent Happening or coming after something else.

terrestrial Of or relating to the Earth or its habitants.

theorem An idea that has been demonstrated as true or is assumed to be demonstrable.

vacuum An empty space in which there is no air or other gas; a space from which all or most of the air has been removed.

velocity The speed and direction of an object or wave.

FOR MORE INFORMATION

American Astronomical Society
2000 Florida Avenue NW
Suite 300
Washington, DC 20009
(202) 328-2010
Website: http://aas.org
The American Astronomical Society (AAS)
   was established in 1899. It is the major
   professional organization in North
   America for astronomers and others
   who have an interest in astronomy.

American Institute of Physics
One Physics Ellipse
College Park, MD 20740
(301) 209-3100
Website: http://www.aip.org
The American Institute of Physics (AIP) is
   a not-for-profit membership corporation
   that promotes the advancement of physics
   and represents thousands of professionals
   and students of the physics community.

Astronomical League
9201 Ward Parkway, Suite 100
Kansas City, MO

(816) 444-4878
Website: http://www.astroleague.org
The goal of the Astronomical League is
to encourage an interest in astronomy throughout the United States
through educational and observational
programs.

Canadian Institute for Advanced Research
180 Dundas Street West, Suite 1400
Toronto, ON M5G 1ZB
Canada
(416)971-4251
Website: http://www.cifar.ca
The Canadian Institute for Advanced
Research (CIFAR) brings together
researchers in a variety of fields for the
purpose of making scientific and techno-
logical strides as well as building stronger
societies, improving the environment,
and much more.

Chicago Astronomical Society
P.O. Box 30287
Chicago, IL 60630
Website: http://www.gadboisproductions
.com/cas
Chicago Astronomical Society (CAS) is the

oldest astronomical society in North America. The organization is dedicated to the advancement of astronomy.

Royal Astronomical Society of Canada
203-4920 Dundas Street West
Toronto, ON M9A 187
Canada
(416) 924-7973
Website: http://www.rasc.ca
The beginnings of the Royal Astronomical Society of Canada (RASC) go back to the middle of the nineteenth century. It aims to further interest in astronomy through its publications, programs, educational outreach, and membership benefits.

WEBSITES

Because of the changing nature of Internet links, Rosen Publishing has developed an online list of websites related to the subject of this book. This site is updated regularly. Please use this link to access the list:

http://www.rosenlinks.com/SCI/Cosm

FOR FURTHER READING

Bortz, Fred. *The Big Bang Theory: Edwin Hubble and the Origins of the Universe*. New York, NY: Rosen Publishing, 2014.

Coles, Peter. *Cosmology*. Oxford, England: Oxford University Press, 2001.

DeVorkin, David, ed. *Beyond Earth*. Washington, DC: National Geographic, 2002.

Fleisher, Paul. *The Big Bang*. Minneapolis, MN: Twenty-First Century Books, 2006.

Krauss, Lawrence, M. *A Universe from Nothing*. New York, NY: Atria Paperback, 2012.

Liddle, Andrew, and Jon Loveday. *Oxford Companion to Cosmology*. Oxford, England: Oxford University Press, 2009.

Liv, Charles. *The Handy Astronomy Answer Book*. Canton, MI: Visible Ink Press, 2008.

Prinja, Raman K., and Richard Iguace. *Understanding the Universe*. New York, NY: Facts on File, Inc., 2002.

Sagan, Carl. *Cosmos*. New York, NY: Ballantine Books, 2013.

Venezia, Mike. *Stephen Hawking*. New York, NY: Children's Press, 2009.

INDEX